Cristian Arnini

We wish you'll like it
Do what you want with this book
Share with the world
Show what you have bought
Next time, spend this money to do something better

IF YOU ARE READING THIS BOOK
YOU ARE PROBABLY
AND YOU HAVE ENOUGH MONEY TO THROW AWAY

**EVERY TIME SOMEBODY BUYS THIS BOOK
A WALLET IN THE WORLD DIES**

THIS BOOK WON'T **TEACH YOU ANYTHING**
YOU CAN SHOW YOUR
HOW **RICH YOU ARE**

IF YOU WANT A DEDICATED **LIBRARY**
CONTACT US
WE WILL YOU

THANK YOU FOR BUYING (NO REFUND PLEASE)
SUGGEST   FANTASTIC BOOK TO ALL YOUR FRIENDS

IF YOU HAVEN'T ALREADY BOUGHT THIS BOOK AND
YOU'RE READING THIS ON A
DON'T WAIT AND GO TO AMAZON TO BUY ONE

this page isn't empty

goodbye man